CRISIS INTERVENTION

THE NEUROBIOLOGY OF CRISIS

DR. JEANNE BROOKS

Elani
PUBLISHING
A PRINT, DIGITAL & TECHNOLOGY COMPANY

www.ElaniPublishing.com
ISBN-13:978-1979421119
ISBN-10:1979421110

CRISIS INTERVENTION

Foreword

This manual is meant to help prepare your agency to perform some of the most challenging work: helping people through crisis. Dr. Brooks has worked in the mental health field for over thirty years with a specialty in crisis, and for the last ten years, she has been training counseling students in crisis intervention. Natural disasters, mass shootings, refugee crises, human sex trafficking, etc. show the growing need for individuals to be prepared to sit with others in their suffering. The need is growing, yet the workers are few. Dr. Brooks has recognized that more and more organizations, disciplines, and ministries are doing crisis intervention with little to no knowledge or understanding of the effects that working with people in crisis has on the crisis worker. This manual will help you gain a better understanding of how trauma effects an individual, as well as how working with people in crisis can affect the interventionist. This information can help you work more effectively by training you and your team members in self-sustainment. This Christian perspective of intervention will help you and your agency become more Christ-like in your approach by instilling a confidence and hope in the most horrific of circumstances, while still maintaining your strong faith in the goodness of God. The preventative practices provided in this manual will help prevent burnout, compassion fatigue, and vicarious trauma for crisis interventionist.

This manual is meant to help individuals who are working with people in crisis. This can be used for mental health professionals or paraprofessionals who work in crisis agencies or ministries. Please note: this manual will not prepare you to deal with crisis such as suicidal or homicidal individuals, nor will it prepare you to work with the chronically mentally ill individual who is in crisis. This manual is designed for outreach to those in a current crisis or trauma due to a natural or manmade disaster. The goal is to help individuals return to their pre-crisis states. If you are not a mental health professional, please make sure you have quick and easy access to mental health professionals in your area so that if there is an actively suicidal or homicidal individual, you will be able to get the individual the help they need. Your agency should have a protocol in place that you can refer to, if, and when, you come in contact with an actively suicidal or homicidal person. If there is not a formal protocol for such a situation, please consider inviting a mental health professional to your organization who can help establish such a protocol. For more information on this, you can reach Dr. Jeanne Brooks at jeanne@drjeannebrooks.com .

DR. JEANNE BROOKS

Crisis Intervention

Neurobiology of Crisis

Crisis Defined

A crisis is an event that presents a real or perceived threat to life or security. This event causes the individual to believe that his/her life or security is in danger, and creates both a physical and emotional reaction that leads to a distressed state. Once an individual is in a state of distress, the physiological response of crisis begins, and the **brain goes into crisis mode.** A person in a state of distress is no longer functioning in a stable realm. This state of distress places a person in a **flight, fight, or freeze mode.** The physiological response of fight/flight/freeze mode prepares the individual to react to this perceived danger. It is a hyper-vigilant/hyper-reactive state where reasoning and rational problem solving are no longer forefront. This distressed fight or flight mode is typically a temporary state of disequilibrium, a temporary state of being hyper-vigilant and hyper-reactive.

The Neurobiology of Crisis:

- The brain in crisis
- Fight/flight/freeze

During a crisis state, an individual is operating out of the limbic system. The limbic system is mid-section of the brain, and includes the amygdala, hippocampus, and hypothalamus.

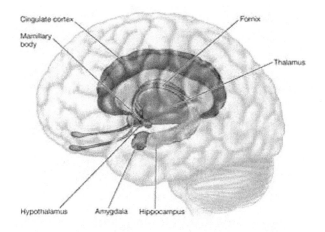

This area of the brain is an important

element to the body's response to stress, and is

highly connected to the endocrine system and the

autonomic nervous system. The associated

functions in the limbic system are: memory

formation, emotion regulation, olfactory

processing, and sexual arousal. When there has

been excessive activation in this area (e.g. long-

term stress or long-term trauma), associated

behavioral responses can be, but are not limited to:

heightened agitation, uncontrolled emotions,

abnormal biological rhythms, abnormal sexual

behavior, and memory impairment.

When a person experiences a crisis, the pituitary glands release adrenaline, cortisol, and dopamine. This causes an increase in heart rate and prepares the person to fight, flight, or, in extreme cases, freeze. It is the body's natural, healthy way to respond to a real threat; however, prolonged exposure to this stress response causes an excessive, ongoing release of cortisol, which can damage brain cells. Prolonged exposure to cortisol has been linked to the breakdown of the hippocampus, which is responsible for memory-making. In addition, excessive cortisol overwhelms and decreases the release of the "feel good" hormones, such as serotonin. When a person is in the midst of crisis, his/her brain is stuck in the limbic system. The longer an individual is stuck in the limbic system, the more at-risk he/she becomes.

There are four specific things that help determine a crisis. As stated earlier, a crisis is an **event** that leads a person to perceive danger (real or not), and the **perception of this danger leads to distress.** It is important to pause and explain that regardless of others' perception of the event, if the individual **perceives it as danger,** the body goes into a crisis mode with the corresponding physiological responses. The body does not discern real or perceived danger, it simply responds to the individual's belief of needing to flee or fight. The body's response then sets the stage for **diminished functioning** directly related to the event. This is a **temporary state of disequilibrium;** it is not the person's typical functioning style. Evidence such as educational background, occupation, daily activities, etc. may help crisis interventionists determine an individual's level of functioning prior to crisis events.

Four Crisis Identifiers

- A precipitating event
- Perception of the event leads to distress
- Diminished functioning when distress is not alleviated with customary coping resources
- A temporary state of disequilibrium

After a crisis state has been identified in an individual, crisis intervention may begin. This initial stage of crisis intervention revolves around stabilization of the individual through assessment and provision of basic needs. Because crises oftentimes involve the loss of basic needs (e.g. food, water, shelter), the first step in crisis intervention is assessing current needs. It may be helpful for the crisis interventionist to ask: are the individual's basic needs being met? If not, what resources are available to help provide these needs? Once basic needs have been identified, the crisis interventionist should assist the individual in meeting these needs, providing 24-hour watch/sitting when necessary.

Remember, this person is in a temporary diminished state of functioning, and can be exhibiting characteristics that are unstable and unsafe. The temporary state of dysfunction can take on clinical features of hostility, disorganization, preoccupation with images, and behavioral changes that can be unpredictable. Until stabilization occurs, the individual may need 24-hour care.

Physiologically, initial stages of crisis intervention are about sitting and helping the person move out of his/her trauma brain, out of the limbic system, and away from the fight or flight mode. It can be helpful to think of this as a reactive state, as the person being stuck in their "reactive brain". If the person has experienced intense trauma or ongoing long-term trauma, this reactive brain can be in overdrive, functioning at a hypersensitive state to everything happening around them, ready to flee or fight. This is a very unpredictable state. The goal is to help the individual operate in a higher functioning area of the brain that is able to reason, make decisions, and emotionally regulate, specifically the Cerebral Cortex.

Sitting

Sitting at the Well: Receiving Restoring and Revealing

One of my favorite stories in the Bible is the

story of Jesus sitting at the well with the Samaritan woman. Although the Samaritan woman was not in a crisis as defined by this manual, the shame, judgment and conviction she felt because of her life choices could have quickly led her to a crisis state. Her perception of others' judgment could have rendered her stuck in her reactive brain, but Jesus sat lovingly with her, an act that changed her projected course. The way Jesus sat with her gives us a perfect example of how to sit with people in crisis.

Job, a person truly in crisis, was not as fortunate. Job's friends came to see Job in his true state of crisis. He had just lost all his wealth, all his children, and his health. His friends were so grieved by the news that they came and "sat with him for seven days and nights. No one said a word to Job, for they saw that his suffering was too great for words" (Job 2:13). Sadly, Job's friends' response to his suffering became far more hurtful than it was edifying once they opened their mouths.

Job's friends' responses clearly indicated they cast great judgment upon Job as they questioned his faith in God, his integrity, and his innocence. Job was already suffering immensely, and their responses only added to his suffering and anguish. Compare the story of Job with the story of the woman at the well. Job's friends responded to Job's innocence with judgement, while Jesus sat with the woman at the well with such compassion that it opened a dialogue of truth.

I believe that Jesus must have sat so filled with love for this woman who was so filled with shame, that it completely changed her. The Samaritan woman was cast out and rejected by her own people, but the King of Kings looked upon her with love, sat with her at the well, and poured living water upon her to restore her. This living water changed her. Job's friends spoke too quickly into Job's suffering without taking the time to listen and understand, **but Jesus loved by sitting well**. Crisis interventionists can learn from these opposing approaches. One approach is to sit in love, while the other is to desperately try to speak into lives with little to no true understanding.

Jesus' act of sitting with the woman at the well was life-changing, **but just as life-changing was her willingness to stay and sit**. This image of just sitting at the well, receiving the living water Christ offered her, is an image that is very powerful to me. Job's friends wanted to quickly speak their opinion of what they believed to be the problem and the solution. All three friends were wrong, but none of them could see their fallacy.

Sadly, individuals oftentimes come to intervene in a crisis thinking they have all the answers and must speak into the situation, when in reality, the individual may just need a calm presence who sits in love while he/she regains some composure.

Jesus' act of sitting well by The Well is a beautiful depiction of what crisis interventionist should do. There is such healing that comes from just sitting with someone as they navigate through their hurt, sorrow, grief, fears, and questions. Sitting well often looks like the ability to sit with a countenance that radiates a confidence for the person in crisis. A confident countenance communicates an understanding that the interventionist believes in the strength within the individual. Jesus must have had that confident countenance, radiating to the woman "you are loved and you can overcome these current circumstances".

Sitting well at The Well allows the interventionist to be freed from the need to fix, or explain why the crisis happened. Sitting well at The Well creates space for knowing where true healing comes from, that the healing is on the way, and that the emotional state of the person in front of you will stabilize. Sadly, what keeps us from sitting well at The Well is the emotional state of the individual in crisis. It can be uncomfortable sitting with others that are in deep despair and pain. Job's friends found it challenging and tried to offer answers. Jesus, on the other hand, sat, loved and acknowledged. Sitting well at The Well requires sitting, loving, and acknowledging the pain and suffering without feeling a need to fix it.

DR. JEANNE BROOKS

The Brain in Crisis

Cerebral Cortex

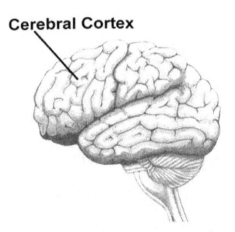

The act of sitting lovingly with a person in crisis offers him/her the ability to enter the area of the brain that is able to reason and self-regulate. More specifically, the frontal and side area of the Cerebral Cortex, the Frontal Lobes, and the Temporal Lobes are the areas of highest functioning. The Cerebral Cortex, including the Prefrontal Cortex (can be referred to as the relational brain), includes both the right (RH)

and left hemisphere (LH). The RH is involved in nonverbal, spatial, and relational functioning. More specifically, the RH is responsible for emotion regulation, spatial processing, creativity, and the ability to process novel environmental cues to perceive them in their entirety, rather than in isolation (i.e. the ability to see the forest through the trees; Fisher, 2014). The LH involves verbal, sequential, and rational functioning. The left hemisphere is essentially responsible for reasoning and logic, taking minute information and discerning it (i.e. looking at the tree in the forest). Both the RH and LH are paramount in daily interaction, and are of utmost importance to developing long-lasting, healthy relationships, hence the term relational brain.

Crisis, Neurobiology and Relationships

It is important for the crisis interventionist to understand the basic dynamics of trauma on the brain. It is equally important for the interventionist to understand how prior crisis/trauma can affect the individual's ability to overcome current crises. Much is reported on abuse and toxic stress on brain development. Long-term, toxic stress redirects the wiring of the brain, creating hypersensitivity to stress and anxiety, and an overdeveloped, reactive brain. Amen (2005) refers to this hypersensitivity as an overactive emotional response, or an overactive limbic system. In addition, research is indicating that the areas of the brain most affected by trauma [Amygdala and other parts of the Limbic system] are the areas that are responsible for connecting [integrating information] to the world around us, processing and retaining that information, and responding to events with proper emotional regulation, all of which involve the higher cortex region (Garner et al., 2012). Chronic stress and trauma can render a brain prone to challenges with attention, impulsivity, disorganization, poor judgment, and conflict seeking, as well as oppositional behavior, aggression, and learning disabilities (Garner et al., 2012), all of which are evidence of underdeveloped neural highways.

One might think of these underdeveloped neural highways as cyclical and stuck in the limbic system. These highways become not so different from a traffic circle, stuck with no exit into the higher cortex areas. Amen (2005) identified that the neural networking in the limbic system becomes over-sensitive to once innocuous stimuli, with no highway system to take the cues to the Somatosensory Cortex and the Orbitofrontal Cortex, the areas of the brain that help make sense of the environment and emotionally self-regulate. Instead, the limbic system highway keeps the individual in an emotional, reactive state, as if true threat and danger are evident. Van der Kolk states that the limbic system is the part of the brain that helps guide emotions and behaviors that are necessary for self-preservation and survival, more specifically, the primitive impulses of the Central Nervous System (2014).

An individual with underdeveloped neural highways into the higher cortex regions of the brain has a difficult time relating to others because he/she is stuck in an emotional, reactive, self-preservation mode. One can see this cyclical, self-preservation mode in child developmental trauma when children do not seek comfort in times of distress, do not calm in times of comforting, and are not emotionally responsive to others' attempts at socialization. As Fisher (2014?) states, the children's behavioral responses are "deeply etched in the brain" (pg.8). If one is stuck in self-preservation mode, one would not trust the behaviors of others because the neuronal messages are conveying that others cannot be trusted, no one is there to truly comfort and provide support, and gentle touches will surely become hurtful touches. These neuronal messages are developed very early based upon the abusive, neglectful environments these children come from. Any new environmental socialization is assimilated into the current neural network, the traffic circle that has no exits, that is reinforced over and over, and that is deeply etched into the reactive brain. There are no highway systems to help reason and logically offer the suggestion that this is a new place, different people who have shown nurturing and loving acts. There are no highway systems from the reactive brain to the relational brain to help logically process new information, to compare this new information with old information, and to establish some sort of social awareness of what can be trusted and what cannot. The only highway system currently functioning well is the highway system of survival and self-preservation.

To further expound on this, it is important to understand the purpose of the Amygdala and how it is connected to the Hippocampus, also located in the Limbic

System. The Amygdala is most specifically responsible for shame, fear, and rage responses, which can easily be considered self-preservation emotions. Sometime these responses are best described as the fight or flight response. When a brain is experiencing healthy development with bonding and attachment, the neural highway begins to formulate through the hippocampus, an area of the brain responsible for memory formation. The hippocampus can be referred to as the memory portal (Fisher, 2014). The highway system then needs to establish itself through the Thalamus, which is heavily involved in relaying information from the limbic system to the higher cortex. The significance of neural connections through this region cannot be overlooked.

Although the Thalamus is a far more complicated structure than this article can properly address, the significance of the role it plays in relaying sensorimotor information from the brainstem and limbic system is imperative to understand for the purpose of this article. This relay station serves as a decoder of information, sending pertinent information to the appropriate areas of the brain. One could say it determines the exits in the traffic circle of the neuronal highway system, taking information from the primitive areas of the brain and driving the information to other areas of the brain. Basically, it helps to discern real danger/threat from innocuous stimuli, a water moccasin as compared to a long black stick. In essence, these neuronal highway exits offer passages out of the self-preservative, reactive brain (limbic system), to the relational brain, or the higher cortex regions that logically and emotionally regulate (Fisher, 2014). Fisher describes the cerebral Cortex as the "thinking cap", stating it is the part of the brain that most differentiates humans from more primitive primates. The Thalamus is responsible for relaying the messages to the relational brain; it is the traffic director allowing the messages to exit the reactive brain and process through to the relational brain.

Effective highway systems from the limbic system to the RH and LH of the Cerebral Cortex are vital to develop long-lasting, healthy relationships. Without a proper exit system out of the reactive brain, information is not able to get to the relational brain, leaving the person trapped in the limbic system with no way to escape (Fisher, 2014). The person caught in this never ending traffic circle with no exits is likely to be constantly pressed with fear, shame, anger, rage, and an overall sense of worthlessness. All external information and environmental stimuli filter through this reactive brain, are irrationally interpreted, and then leave the individual to respond reactively, with little to no emotional regulation.

A phenomenon that is evident in an underdeveloped or inactive relational brain is a lack of empathy or emotional intelligence (EI). In 1995 Daniel Goleman began refining the concept of emotional intelligence. Since then, he has been formulating this reality with the most recent neuroscience research, gleaning even more support for the importance of emotional intelligence. EI is best defined as the ability to "be aware of, control, and express one's emotions, and to handle interpersonal relationships judiciously and empathetically; it is recognized as the key to both personal and professional success" (English Oxford Living Dictionary, 2017). Unique brain centers have been linked to EI that are separate from the brain centers associated with IQ.

The brain centers that are most activated in EI are the Amygdala, the Anterior Cingulate, the right brain Somatosensory Cortex and the Orbitofrontal Cortex. The Amygdala is the part of the limbic system that is responsible in processing fear and emotions. Its basic function is to link areas of higher functioning to areas of lower metabolic function, like the hypothalamus and the brain stem. The Anterior Cingulate is the frontal region of the Cingulate Gyrus, another part of the limbic system that helps drive the conscious thought of unpleasant experiences. Most specifically, it is involved in processing the reality of fear-based experiences. The Somatosensory Cortex is found in the higher cortex mid-section of the brain, and is responsible for sensory processing and integration. The Orbitofrontal Cortex is part of the frontal cortex, the area of the brain that is considered to be responsible for higher brain functions. The Orbitofrontal cortex is in the far front, right above the orbits of the eyes. This area of the brain is critical for executive function, emotional regulation, and reasoning; essentially, it is responsible for emotional decision-making.

For EI to fully develop, it requires the integration of the limbic system (Amygdala and Anterior Cingulate), and the higher cortex regions (Somatosensory Cortex and the Orbitofrontal Cortex). This integration requires the neural highways to fully and adequately develop. The brain stem and the limbic system are well in place at birth, however, the higher level cortexes of the brain require further development through the infant's interaction with the world. The relational brain develops through bonding and attachment, and through the relationship of the caregiver to the infant. The give and take of social cues such as smiling, laughing, cooing, and talking helps the highways develop. Without relational interacting, the neural highways end up underdeveloped or not developed at all. With an underdeveloped relational brain, one may have underdeveloped EI. With little to no development of the neural highways, one may suffer from Reactive Attachment Disorder (RAD).

Early crisis intervention is extremely important for helping individuals respond in an emotionally regulated, as opposed to an emotionally reactive manner. Physiologically, to help a person out of the reactive brain (fight or flight region), one must spend time helping them move into their emotionally regulated, reasoning brain, as well as help them learn to trust and respond to the safety that surrounds them. In essence, the crisis interventionist helps those in crisis out of their reactive brain by sitting with them in a calm, attentive manner, and assists them in processing in their higher cortex region, their relational brain. When a person is in a crisis state, the clinical features of the reactive brain are; **somatic distress, feelings of guilt, hostility, disorganization, behavioral changes, and preoccupation of images.** Early intervention offers an escape from the reactive brain into the relational brain, decreasing the risk of the individual suffering more long term effects of a constant state of fear, shame, anger, rage, and feelings of worthlessness.

Clinical Features of Crisis:

- Somatic distress
- Feeling of guilt
- Hostility
- Disorganization
- Behavioral changes
- Preoccupation with images

Prolonged states of crisis can become neurologically damaging, and can affect the person's overall long-term functioning. Of the many types of trauma victims that can be explored, RAD and PTSD are two disorders most often equated to the high-jacking of the limbic system. Both disorders are related to significant trauma. RAD displays developmental, ongoing trauma, while PTSD can present after one very significant trauma, such as an assault that goes untreated. The brain's reaction to PTSD can be best described as the trauma event being tattooed into the limbic system, imprinted so deeply that the individual becomes stuck in the reactive brain. Fisher (2014) states, "we have seen that implicit memory of trauma and neglect are held in the dysregulated amygdala and hippocampus...and that this memory is sustained as dysrhythmic, habitual patterns in electrical neural networks [highways] that hum [caught in a traffic circle] with information and misinformation" (pg. 78). With significant, ongoing trauma for which there is no perceived escape or help, whatever highway system may have been developed can be destroyed or severely damaged, leaving the person locked in the reactive brain. Examples of ongoing trauma with no perceived escape or help include Battered Wife syndrome or Stockholm syndrome. To date, Battered Wife Syndrome is a recognized disorder with an ICD code, however Stockholm syndrome has no agreed upon diagnostic criteria, therefore it does not appear as a formal diagnosis.

RAD, PTSD, Battered Wife Syndrome, and Stockholm syndrome all are related to trauma, all have significant symptoms that strongly indicate a deficit in the ability to self-regulate, reason, and process information logically, and all are reactive in nature. Evidence suggests that RAD and PTSD individuals are hypersensitive to stress and have an overactive stress response (fight or flight), both of which occur in the limbic system (Amen, 2005). The advancement of neuroscience and imaging of the brain shows a concentration of activity in the limbic system, and the lack of activity in the prefrontal region, suggesting poor or ineffective neuro-highways from the limbic system to the frontal region. Advancements in neurofeedback are showing great promises in the development of the highways in RAD children. "The brains of these patients learn to forgo habitual patterns [exits out of the reactive brain begin forming], and the patients become less susceptible to a stress response and have many more choices in how they respond to a stressor when it occurs [they find themselves in the relational brain]. Neurofeedback raises the brains threshold to stress and generally increases stress resilience as it increases stability" (Fisher, 2014, Pg 79). Neurofeedback helps generate or regenerate healthy neuro-highway systems, representing the plasticity of the brain that we are beginning to respect (Fisher, 2014; Amen, 2005; Thompson

2010). This new science indicates that the brain is capable of regeneration, that those affected by trauma can be more resilient than we once thought, and that early intervention is extremely important.

When Crisis Becomes Critical:

- PTSD
- Toxic Stress (RAD, Battered Wife Syndrome, Stockholm Syndrome)

It is essential to understand the effects ongoing trauma has on the brain, specifically the person's inability to access the relational brain. When the crisis interventionist understands that the individual's highway systems were not built to transport information from the reactive brain to the relational brain, patience and understanding flow more naturally into client care. Emotion regulation and high emotional intelligence (EQ) are of great importance when working with an individual that has been high-jacked in the reactive brain (Fisher, 2014). Great patience is needed when working with individuals that suffer developmental trauma and/or have a history of ongoing trauma as building the foundational structures for new neural highways can be very time consuming. These communication highway systems are complicated and can take years to develop. Patience and perseverance from the crisis interventionist allow highways systems to develop fully, leaving time and space for those that do not have a thoroughfare yet. Without a fully developed highway system that goes from the reactive brain to the relational brain, the trauma victim will continue to respond reactively. Highway systems may still be under construction as the trauma victim learns to trust. As trust is built between the trauma victim and interventionist, bonding may occur, even without evidence of the person's changed behavior. If the care giver quits, whatever highway system was being developed may be destroyed, validating the trauma victim's reactive brain as it repeats, "There is no one I can trust."

With respect to understanding trauma and the brain, the new insights to neuroscience offer a tremendous opportunity to begin looking at other social and psychological phenomenon and treatment interventions differently. Embracing the importance of the balance between the RH and LH (relational brain), and the power the reactive brain has to interfere with one's ability to access the relational brain can help treatment providers and caregivers find a way to better approach the reactive person. Goleman (2011) speaks of the high-jacking of the limbic system and how it interferes with EQ. Goleman speaks of EQ and how it is related to the Prefrontal Cortex, both RH and LH. EQ is needed in the development of healthy, long-lasting relationships, and is seen more and more as a desired ability for employees. Individuals that suffer from RAD are identified with having low EQ. Low EQ, RAD, PTSD, and other trauma-related disorders are all connected to the high-jacking of the limbic system with poor access to the emotional regulation and rational thinking that is evident of Prefrontal Cortex abilities. In essence, gaining respect for the importance of cultivating an active relational brain can have a significant impact on many of the current issues seen in the offices of treatment providers. Now that it is evident that the brain is plastic and new neural highways can be developed, our treatment must follow suit.

Long-term Neurological Effects of Untreated Crisis:

- Executive functioning impairment
- Poor self-regulation
- Low EQ

The Neurobiology of Sitting at The Well

I shared the concept of "sitting at the Well." This concept is basically the idea of receiving the love of Christ in such a way that it restores us and renews us. This allows us the ability to sit with others as they receive, are restored, and are renewed. To sit with others we must first sit, and it is in this act of sitting that we find peace. There is a neurological phenomenon of peace, but there is also the neurological phenomenon of anxiety and fear that can sometimes overpower our neurological peace. The act of sitting at the Well is an act of finding that neurological peace. To get that neurological peace that surpasses all understanding, one must first find peace with the Lord, for it is only drawing closer to the Lord that can settle our fears and shame. He is the one who can calm our anxious spirit. Anxiousness comes from our experiences of shame and guilt, but the act of sitting at The Well and receiving living water from our Savior has the ability to wash over all the shame, guilt, and fear we become riddled with.

There is a profound neurological difference in the act of focusing on our Savior's ability to wash us clean from our shame (sitting), and living in fear and shame. Neurologically, it takes a greater intellectual ability, and a higher level of thinking, to concentrate on the truth of our Savior's ability to wash us clean than it does to stay stuck in fear and shame. This ability to reason in our higher cortex, to logically think through truths and create long-lasting, loving relationships, is an ability that God created just for us so we could come to know Him and hold firm to His truths.

This act of sitting at The Well, receiving the love of our Savior, focusing on His truths, requires us to be active in our frontal cortex area of the brain, as compared to being stuck in our limbic system, the reactive area of the brain. The limbic system is also known as the "go" area, or the area of the brain that is responsible for a quick reaction that protects us from harm or danger. The limbic system is a great system when there is true danger, but is not as helpful when danger is perceived rather than real.

The highly stressed or traumatized brain can misread external signals as danger, setting in motion a very quick reaction without much logic to counteract the shame that is driving the reaction. It is amazing how shame affects the brain. Shame is the belief that there is something innately bad/wrong with us. Shame can define us and define how we relate to one another. Shame is the result of what has happened to us and/or the choices we have made. Guilt is an emotion that warns us when what we are *doing* is wrong, shame is a state of being that says who we *are* is wrong. Guilt guides us to adjust and change, shame guides us to cower and hide.

Shame drives the limbic system to perceive danger where there is none, setting the entire neurological system to "go" as if there were imminent danger. When we are operating out of this "go" system we are most certainly in a fight or flight mode, responding to everything around us as if we must run or fight. When we are stuck in this neurological loop, we are unable to sit well at The Well, by not responding to others well. Remember we are in a "go" mode which will cause us to fight or flight, and who wants to sit with someone who is in a fight or flight mode?

It is imperative that we first sit at The Well with our Savior, allowing Him to settle our "go" part of the brain, and allowing Him to show us how not to react to one another by fighting or running. When we sit well, we are free to focus on the truths of who He is, how much He loves us, and how to love others as He loves us.

Sitting at The Well, focusing on these truths, helps us out of the limbic system by settling us, causing us to lose the desire to run or fight. Sitting at The Well allows us to move into our logical, emotionally regulating brain, and to receive His love, letting it wash over us, allowing us to feel calmer. The calmer we feel, the more we can focus on who He really is. The more we focus on who He really is, reminding ourselves of His truths, the calmer we are. The more we sit with Him, breathing in all of who He was and is, the less fear and shame we feel. We are free to focus on the truth that there is no guilt or shame that is bigger than the cross. His death covered all that has happened to us and what we have done. There is not one thing that the cross cannot heal.

He took it all to the cross, carrying it to the grave, and not one thing is too big for the cross. Spending time in the word, acknowledging that His truths cover it all, and praising and worshiping Him helps us get out of that limbic system loop of shame, fear, and anxiety. Sitting and breathing it all in neurologically helps us out of our "go" brain and allows us to get into the higher cortex region of the relational brain where we are no longer reactive to the things around us, but can rest on His truths and receive His love.

After we have received His love and allowed ourselves to be present in the relational, higher cortex region of our brain, we are far better able to reveal who He is to others. When we are emotionally regulating and focusing on truths His truths, we are far better able to sit well at The Well with others. Sitting well with others allows for a renewal of who we are to be as a church, as a body of believers who love God first and others second, and who are no longer riddled with self-deprecating, self-preservative behaviors that push others away.

Beware, there is an enemy that has been working overtime in keeping us captive in the limbic system. This enemy wants us stuck in shame and fear. He wants us to react to one another in hostility, judgment and isolation so that we cannot meet Jesus at The Well. The devil wants to hold us hostage in the reactive brain, believing his lies and doubting God. The enemy entraps and isolates us, keeping us in the dark and causing us to be afraid of the light and the truth. The enemy wants us to believe that we are our shame and God's love is not for us. The devil wants us to believe his lies and doubt others. The enemy wants us to believe that our brothers and sisters are our enemies. The enemy stimulates us to react to one another with hostility and fear and has created many different avenues that drive us to this reactive area of the brain. The enemy uses divisive measures to cause us to doubt one another, triggering our shame so we stay stuck in the cycle of reactivity, fighting or running from one another with little time to slow down and reason through truths. This inability to stay focused on logic keeps us emotionally irregulated, reacting impulsively with one another. The enemy is causing our thoughts to go round and round the anxious, agitated cycle of distrust and animosity, but our Savior is at The Well, waiting patiently.

Our Savior is waiting to offer us the living water that washes away all these doubts and fears, waiting to help us focus on Him, on His love, and on His truths that will settle us. We just need to take the time to come to The Well and sit, receive, and be restored. Once we are restored and renewed, we can be used to help others find restoration and renewal.

The Crisis Worker

Crisis intervention can be stressful. Working

and sitting with others in crisis can be overwhelming. It is imperative for the interventionist to be calm, not reactive, when sitting with someone in crisis. Stress management is of utmost importance in the field of crisis intervention due to the added stress of working with people in crisis. A reactive brain can trigger a reactive brain, so it is important to be able to manage that reactive potential. Without proper management, crisis interventionists are at high risk of **countertransference, burnout, compassion fatigue**, or **vicarious trauma.**

Countertransference is the emotional entanglement that can happen when working with severely traumatized or abused individuals. When the interventionist has unresolved trauma in his/her own life, a crisis brain can trigger a crisis brain, meaning listening to another person's crisis can stir memories of one's own crisis. When this happens, the interventionist can become overinvolved and can over-identify with the victim. The interventionist begins using the intervention as a means to fulfill their own unmet needs in their time of crisis. The phenomenon of countertransference is a perfect example of why it is so important for interventionists to make sure they have faced their own issues of hurt, brokenness, and healing. Once one has walked through the valley of suffering and found healing, it gives them an even better ability to walk with someone else in the midst of suffering. Once one truly *knows* healing and comes out of suffering stronger, that person can walk alongside another in a confidence that only comes from KNOWING.

Burnout and Compassion Fatigue are the results of the interventionist not properly caring for themselves. Sitting and hearing the trauma that others go through can cause a compassionate heart to desire to take in and fix an individual's wounds. It is as if the interventionist begins taking on the responsibility of the victims healing, and taking too much responsibility for the victim's life and recovery. It is very important for the interventionist to maintain healthy professional boundaries while still being compassionate and caring. Neglecting proper boundaries and believing that one is responsible for the complete healing and restoration of another leads to a weariness and exhaustion that is both physical and emotional. Burnout is cumulative, and over time can lead to a numbness and detachment from others' sorrows, also known as compassion fatigue. Boundaries allow the interventionist to realize the significance of caring without taking on the responsibility of healing. When one embraces the significance of caring, one can sit with the victim, assisting them and empowering them to become an active part of their own healing.

Vicarious Trauma is a phenomenon in which victims' trauma stories heard over and over begin to alter the interventionists way of thinking. The stories of others' traumas begin to create trauma for the interventionist. Crisis interventionists are at high risk of vicarious trauma because of the continual exposure to the persistent stories of trauma they are exposed to.

Risk Factors to Working with the Persons in Crisis

- Countertransference
- Burnout
- Compassion fatigue
- Vicarious Trauma

Preventative Care

When working in constant crisis situations, it is important to create built-in preventative care for countertransference, burnout, compassion fatigue, and vicarious trauma. First and foremost, for every crisis interventionist, it is of utmost importance to first reach out to someone who can help you process through any unresolved trauma. Find healing for the wounds exist because of that trauma. Do not attempt to help others with the belief that by helping others you will find healing. If you are anticipating your own healing coming from their healing, you will put undue pressure on them to heal so you can heal. Instead, reach out and find someone to walk with you in the healing of your trauma. Then you will be able to someday walk with another in the healing of their trauma. Remember, a reactive brain triggers a reactive brain, trauma triggers trauma. So, your unhealed trauma can be triggered by someone else's current trauma.

Secondly, the importance of self-care cannot be overstated. To combat burnout and compassion fatigue, an interventionist must practice good self-care skills. Oftentimes, compassionate people have the hardest time being compassionate to themselves. A good rule of thumb is to practice what one preaches. In crisis intervention, it is important to assess basic needs, emotional needs, physical needs, social needs, and spiritual needs. Practicing what one preaches is to **self-assess** one's own basic needs (proper diet and sleep), emotional (processing through all the stories heard), physical (exercise and diet), social (power of laughter and play) and spiritual (what is the higher purpose). The interventionist must

know themselves and **evaluate their own care**.

- Emotional needs

- Mental

- Physical needs

- Social needs

- Spiritual needs

Emotional needs

First make sure you spend time with someone trained to help you find healing in your trauma. As stated earlier, if you have a history of trauma, then make sure you seek help and healing. The history of trauma does NOT make you inept for this work, but it can render you ineffective. Trauma brain triggers trauma brain, so if you are predisposed to a hyperactive limbic system, a reactive brain, then doing outreach puts you at high risk of becoming reactive when interacting with someone in a crisis state. The act of finding healing gives you a confidence when sitting with others in their crisis state that this state of trauma is just that, a temporary state that can be calmed and healed. Healing does not mean forgotten, so do not confuse the two. But healing does mean that when one remembers the crisis/trauma, they will not resort back to a crisis state...a state of imbalance and reactivity. Healing allows space for peace and understanding that the trauma was survived when memories arise. A crisis brain says survival is questionable; a healed brain says that survival happened and strength was realized. So first, find that calming, peace-filled state for yourself.

Secondly, to maintain good emotional health, one must understand that sitting for long or extended periods of time with others in crisis can become trauma for the worker. This is what was referred to earlier as secondary trauma. Many of us are visual beings, so we create pictures in our heads about the stories others tell us. Those pictures flashed over and over again can create a crisis reaction. Remember, the limbic system does not distinguish between real or imagined. So as those pictures play over in your head, the limbic system can be triggered. Debriefings after outreach serve as a preventative measure to secondary trauma. Debriefing should occur after every outreach, even if you "believe" the current outreach was uneventful. Working in crisis situations regularly causes us to be desensitized to what others would define as eventful. This means you are NOT a good judge as to whether or not the outreach was uneventful. Debrief always.

Debriefing

A debriefing consists of several steps.

Step 1. Introduction – explain the importance of processing through and invite everyone to participate.

Step 2. Facts - everyone share their view of what happened

Step 3. Thoughts – "what was your first thought or most prominent thoughts when you realized what was happening?"

Step 4. Reactions – "what was the very worst thing about the event?" "what were your greatest fears"

Step 5. Symptoms – "what cognitive, physical, emotional, or behavioral symptom are repetitive right now since the event?"

Step 6. Teaching – normalize the thoughts and feeling and give some signs/symptoms to be aware of; sleeping habits changed, not being able to stop thinking about it, eating habits changed, night mares, isolating, not

enjoying activities that usually bring joy,

easily agitated.

Step 7. Re-entry – allow participants to ask

clarifying questions and leave with

encouraging and validating statements

In going through this process, you are

neurologically addressing what the limbic system

first believed, then going into the higher cortex

region to determine what actually happened. This

act of allowing the limbic system to calm, and

leaving the experiences settled in the higher cortex

region of the brain prevents an over-reactive,

hypersensitive limbic system.

What are your emotional needs?

_____

_____

_____

How are you meeting your emotional needs?

What do you need to do differently?

_____

_____

_____

_____

_____

_____

_____

_____

_____

Mental Needs

Mentally, we must determine what we are setting our mind on, and what do we spend much of our time thinking about, telling ourselves, and believing? It is amazing how what we think can become our reality, even when there is no concrete evidence for that reality. Interactions with others can be directly affected by our thoughts. A belief that someone is angry with us or does not like us becomes our reality just because we thought it, but the REALITY may be that the person we are accusing of being mad or not liking us may in fact be a very shy person or a person with a heavy heart about something. We may just be misreading their body language. Thinking they are mad or do not like us leads us to respond to them as if our thoughts are facts, and pushes them away.

The above example shows how our thoughts affect us in the most basic of behaviors. Research is showing that negative thoughts impact the brain. In fact, research shows that our thoughts, what we set our mind on, influences the architecture of our brains. Negative thoughts create unhealthy wiring in our brain that can directly impact our health, while positive thinking improves our overall functioning in our world. In essence, our thoughts become who we are, what we do, and how we feel. What do you set your thoughts on?

_____

_____

_____

_____

_____

_____

_____

_____

_____

_____

How can you change your thought life to a positive thought life?

_____

_____

_____

_____

_____

_____

_____

_____

_____

_____

What do you need to do differently?

_____

_____

_____

_____

_____

_____

_____

_____

Physical Needs

Physically, we must be taking proper care of our bodies. Our bodies operate best when they are balanced through proper diet, exercise, and sleep. A balanced diet includes proteins, fruits, and vegetables, with limits on simple sugars and caffeine. Simple sugars are what we call sweets like candies, cookies, and cake. Complex sugars are carbohydrates and fruits. We need some complex sugars, within reason. Caffeine and other mood altering chemicals must be taken in very small amounts. It may be best to restrict intake in high-stress situations. Mood altering chemicals like alcohol or drugs can make behavior erratic and unpredictable. When working in crisis situations, the interventionist needs to be emotionally stable.

Exercise helps keep the body strong and fit. Stress can create havoc on the digestive system and the ability for the body to burn fats. Fats are not bad for us; in fact, healthy fats are needed in moderation as a source energy. Stress, however, can cause the breakdown of fats to slow. Exercise allows us to keep our bodies fit, strong, and processing foods well. We are meant to be active beings.

Sleep is important; our bodies need rest. Most people need 6-8 hours of sleep a day. There may be a variation for some, but generally, if you are not getting 6-8 hours a day, you may not be getting enough sleep. Lack of sleep will affect your mental processes and increase your stress. If you do not have time to get a good night's sleep on a regular basis, then you are TOO busy and are not

managing your own stress!!!

What are your physical needs?

_____

_____

_____

_____

_____

_____

_____

_____

_____

How are you meeting your physical needs?

_____

_____

_____

_____

What do you need to do differently?

Social Needs

Outreach and ministry cannot be considered your social outlet. Research has shown that laughter and play go a long way in helping to manage stress. Sadly, too many put social outlets and play time on the back-burner thinking there is little significance for, or feeling guilty for having fun. Laughter increases the digestive system, helps the flow of oxygen to the brain, and helps regulate the heart rate. Good social outlets allow us to keep things in perspective. Spending too much of our time working with others in crisis can cloud our perspective, causing us to think that all is a crisis. Healthy social outlets help us stay connected with the goodness in the world.

The key word is "healthy" social outlets. If your personal life is riddled with unhealthy individuals, then you are inviting more crisis into your life. As I stated earlier, it is important to practice what you preach. Chances are, you encourage those you help to get out of unhealthy environments and surround themselves with healthy individuals. Make sure you are doing those same things. Surround yourself with others that encourage you, lift you, and challenge you in encouraging and lifting ways.

Ask yourself, what makes you laugh? Who are the people that when you are with them you feel lighter, happy, and filled with joy, or more peaceful and calm? What are things you like to do that help you focus on the goodness in life? Get rid of the things in your personal life that cause you to feel bitter and stressed. Get rid of things in your personal life that create bad habits or rob you of your peace.

Things that create calm for many are

coloring, walking outside in nature, listening to edifying music, watching a funny movie, spending a nice quiet evening with those you love. Things that can create more stress and anxiety are too much time on social media, gaming, and isolating. Remember, healthy fellowship is good for the soul. What are your social needs?

_____

_____

_____

_____

_____

_____

_____

_____

_____

_____

How are you meeting your social needs?

What do you need to do differently?

Spiritual Needs

Many people join outreach ministry to be the hands and feet of Jesus. We are certainly called to be salt and light to the world, but I find that many of us, after years of ministry, come to forget who the source of the light is, and we lose our salty flavor. We no longer take the time to plug into the source of light, and burn out.

I believe that we are called to do outreach. I believe we are to be the hands and feet of our Lord and Savior. I believe that it is in the outreach, the sitting with others in crisis, that God uses us to share the love of Christ. One of my favorite stories in the Bible is the story of Jesus sitting at the well with the Samaritan woman. I believe that in asking us to be the hands and feet, He is essentially asking us to sit with others who are hurting and filled with shame. There is such a neurological significance I find in that simple act of sitting, especially sitting with the traumatized soul in crisis. I think of the Samaritan woman, the woman Jesus sat with, and consider her crisis of shame and the trauma of being an outcast.

I love the image of Jesus sitting with her and I believe that He must have been so filled with love for this woman who was so filled with shame that it completely changed her. There is significance in the ability to sit with others at The Well, loving them as Christ loves us, and finding that position of truly being the hands and feet of Christ. But, I think our lives can be so hectic "doing ministry" that we very rarely just sit. Many of us have a hard time slowing down enough to take a breath, let alone sit. I think many of us just go, go, go, and are doing, doing, doing "for Christ," trying to be THE light that, our light fades at the end of the day. I believe many of us forget to plug into the source; we fail to sit at The Well with Him to allow Him to fill us again. If we do give ourselves a moment to sit, do we remember to sit with Him, breathing Him in so He can fill us again? We cannot overflow to others without sitting well first.

To be hands and feet for Jesus, we must first sit *with* Jesus. We must sit with His love, sit with His truths, and sit and receive His living water. Do not allow the trappings of your ministry to keep you so busy that you do not allow yourself to sit and breathe in His goodness for you. Sit and spend time reflecting who Jesus is and what He has done for so many before you. Sit and breathe in the truth that He wants to offer you the exact same cleansing as He has for all others.

Be refreshed by this reality of sitting and breathing in our Savior's love for you. Allow this love to pour over you, reviving you for great and glorious things. Let our Lord of Lord's love restore you to do the work God created you to do, but with His help. Let this act of sitting restore you, to refresh you.

May we all learn to sit at The Well, well, and receive His love. May we be restored and reveal His love to others. It is imperative that we do not lose the proper perspective in outreach for others. We must first make sure we are allowing the Father to fill our cup to overflowing, that we plug into the source, so THE SOURCE can radiate His light to a dark world. As individuals, we do not have the ability, on our own accord, to be an eternal source of light. We do, however, have the ability to be plugged into the source.

So, make sure you are spending daily time plugged in, sitting with, and breathing in His love. Make sure you are allowing Him to fill you to overflowing. C.S. Lewis writes, "God made us: invented us as a man invents an engine. A car is made to run on petrol, and it would not run properly on anything else. Now God designed the human machine to run on Himself. He Himself is the fuel our spirits were designed to burn, or the food our spirits were designed to feed on. There is no other." The reality is, if we are not constantly feeding ourselves on our Heavenly Father's word there is an enemy waiting to feed on us.

What are your spiritual needs?

_____

_____

_____

_____

_____

_____

_____

_____

_____

_____

How are you meeting your spiritual needs?

_____

_____

_____

_____

_____

_____

_____

_____

_____

What do you need to do differently?

_____

_____

_____

_____

_____

_____

_____

_____

_____

_____

The Neurobiology of Spiritual Warfare

We all have an enemy lurking, waiting to feed on us. The enemy is particularly interested in destroying God's army of soldiers and ambassadors. The more work you are doing for the Lord, the more persistent the devil is. Dr.

David Jeremiah has a great book, *The Spiritual Warfare Answer Book*. In it, He clearly explains the tactics of the devil and the strategic ways the devil uses to steal, destroy, and kill. Dr. Jeremiah quotes John Phillips, "But our real enemy lurks in the shadows of the unseen world, moving people as pawns on the chessboard of time. As long as we see people as enemies and wrestle with them, we will spend our strength in vain." The devil's main purpose is to destroy our witness and to render us useless in furthering God's eternal Kingdom. God calls us to love one another as He loves us. He calls us to be anxious for nothing, but prayerful and thankful for all things, setting our minds on His truths and His love (Philippians 4:6-9).

Paul writes in Galatians 5 that we are not to become conceited, to provoke one another, or to be jealous of one another. He talks about the fruits of the Spirit; peace, joy, love, goodness, gentleness, kindness, patience, self-control and faithfulness, but, he also warns us against the sinful nature of mankind stating that hostility, outbursts of anger, selfish ambition, dissension, division, and envy are just a few of the realities that we are acting outside of how God would have us behave. I find it poignant that the devil's ways of using us as pawns in his warfare is through deceit, divineness, and destruction.

The devil destroys our ability to exhibit the fruits of the Holy Spirit when he uses us as pawns, causing us to wrestle with others. All it takes is one word out of context to trigger one's insecurities, pride, or self-righteousness. In ministry, this can be seen between workers. The devil wants to divide and conquer. If he can wear the team down, then he has the ability to diminish the effectiveness of the ministry. The devil is a very crafty enemy; he has been studying us, and he knows our vulnerabilities. He is lurking in the dark, just waiting to pounce on our pride or shame, that we may become reactive. **Reactivity triggers reactivity**. We are prone to react to one another, which is why the Bible is so explicit on how to NOT be reactive. The Bible gives us warning after warning, "be slow to anger, slow to speak, and quick to listen" (James 1:19), "be still and know I am God" (Psalm 46:10), "be directed by the Holy Spirit" (Ephesians 5:18), "be humble and gentle " (Ephesians 4:2), "make every effort to keep united by the Spirit" (Ephesians 4:3), "be kind to each other, tenderhearted, forgiving one another, just as God through Christ has forgiven you,"(Ephesians 4:32). These are just a few examples from Paul's writings. There are many more throughout the Bible from the Old Testament (Psalms and Proverbs) and the New Testament. Proverbs is full of warnings against pride, and speaks clearly of how we are to act toward one another.

God has many warnings and guidelines for how we are to be with one another so we can be witnesses to His glory, His love, and His perfect plan for us. God gave us Jesus Christ, He allowed Jesus to walk amongst us to show us how to love one another, how to be slow to speak and slow to anger, and how to be humble. We are asked, as Christ followers, to behave in such a manner, and not to succumb to the trappings of this world so we may witness to the ends of the world. God requires us to be set apart from the things of this world, warns us not to grow anxious, and teaches us not to be prideful. When our actions are set apart, others come to be curious as to what we have they do not. God asks us, even requires us, to learn to sit well at The Well. As I wrote in the Neurobiology of Sitting Well I explained it takes a higher level of intellect to do so.

The devil's ploy is to keep us away from that higher level of intellectual process. **The enemy wants to keep us entrapped in our reactive brain, our limbic system.** The limbic system is the area of the brain that registers a threat and sets our body in a "go motion" setting us to react. In this reactive mode, there is little room for reason, logic, or emotional regulation. Instead, we are set in a primal place of reacting very quickly to what is perceived as a threat. This area of the brain works well when there is a real threat; it sets our body in motion to respond very quickly without having to think through what we are doing. Anyone who has come VERY close to a car wreck has experienced the limbic system at its best.

The problem is, our limbic system alone cannot determine a real threat as compared to a perceived threat. The hippocampus and amygdala help process real vs. perceived threat. These structures are actually on the outer edges of the limbic system. A well-formed limbic system allows for a level of "slow to anger, slow to speak" while quickly processing real as compared to perceived threats. In essence, God created us in such a beautifully complicated way that we are given the ability, unlike other animals, to processing external information relationally. We have been given the capacity to be encouraging and edifying rather than reactive, divisive, and destructive.

But the devil, our only true enemy, has an ability to wreak havoc on our limbic system. An overactive limbic system is an anxious, agitated brain. Neurologically speaking, if we are left in our limbic system too long by prolonged exposure to stress, crisis, or trauma, we begin to have a hypersensitive, reactive brain. It takes less external stimulation to get us reacting to the outside world. The more reactive we are, the less relational we are. The less relational we are, the more divisive we are. The best way for the enemy to destroy and conquer is by dividing the army, by isolating warriors, and by creating so much noise that there is mass chaos and mayhem. The devil has done a beautiful job at isolating and dividing the Body of Christ by first causing us to be SO busy.

We have become too busy to sit and fellowship. Our churches have become so big that we are lost in the sea of faces, and our lives have become so busy we spend very little time sitting with one another. When we are isolated, all we have is ourselves. The body is not working as it should by encouraging and lifting one another, reminding one another of God's goodness and promises. We are not reminding one another of His faithfulness, therefore we are less inclined to set our minds on what is true about Him, and more likely to be drawn into what the world says is true. This Christian walk takes faith, but we begin to lose faith when we are overly focused on the world. We are warned to be in the world but not of it, yet the devil has created such a divisive ploy in the body of believers that it is far too easy to become overwhelmed by the things of this world. There is great purpose in being deliberate in fellowshipping with one another. Sadly, though, the devil can create dynamics that cause so much busyness like working for God, reaching out to others, and pouring out, that we are often left empty.

We find ourselves overwhelmed, anxious, and exhausted, leaving us trapped in our limbic systems, our reactive brain. He then lies to us by making us believe that we are staying connected by social media and electronic communication. He lies to us by causing us to believe that this type of interacting is sufficient for cultivating and nourishing relationships. We buy into the lie that we are just too busy to take the time to actually talk to someone, to have a verbal exchange that requires a far higher level of intellect than the electronic deliverance of information. We have bought into the lie that Facebooking and texting is a sufficient form of communication and can edify the body.

The TRUTH is this form of interacting is

literally just a form of basic data processing. This form of interacting is about delivering and retrieving data. It does not require engagement of the frontal higher cortex that is used in the act of relating and sitting with others. This higher cortex area of the brain helps us grow in our emotional intelligence. Emotional intelligence is what allows us to empathize, truly relate to others, and emotionally regulate. This area of the brain allows us to be relational, not reactive. Empathy allows us to sit with one another, even if we disagree with one another, and listen. It is the ability to place ourselves in another's shoes. It is the ability to see another perspective rather than believing our own perspective is the ONLY truth. It allows us to better walk through conflict without devouring and destroying each other.

The enemy, though, he wants us to destroy

and devour each other. He wants to use us as his pawns, moving us around on the chessboard of life attacking each other "in the name of Christ" so that the world sees us as no different, or maybe even worse than, the world. The devil is using our limbic system, holding us hostage in our reactive brain, so that we lose our ability to be salt and light to this world.

Standing Strong

The devil attacks on several levels, but I like to refer to them as the five D's: Doubt, Discouragement, Delay, Divisiveness, Diversion. He attacks our limbic system with these five D's causing us to slow down and focus on fear, rather than the promises God has given us. The more God is using us, the more persistent the devil is. The more tired we become, the louder he becomes.

How does the devil exploit me with his ploys, the five D's?

_____

_____

_____

_____

_____

_____

_____

_____

_____

Doubt

_____

_____

_____

_____

_____

Discouragement

Delay

Divisiveness

Diversion

What are God's truths compared to the devils lies?

How can I use them against the five D's?

Doubt

Discouragement

Delay

Divisiveness

Diversion

What do you need to do differently to stand

strong?

_____

_____

_____

Crisis Intervention Agencies

Crisis intervention agencies must put safeguards into place for workers so they do not become victims to their limbic systems and the devil's ploys. Becoming trapped in the limbic system leads to burn out, compassion fatigue, and vicarious trauma. Safeguards must be established by limiting the number of trauma victims each worker is seeing, proper supervision and debriefing, adequate trauma training, and encouragement of self-care for all workers. The more supportive the agency is to **supervision**, **support** and **counseling** for workers, the higher the functioning of the crisis workers.

Directors, practice what you preach. Model the proper self-care and encourage it. Share the ways you manage your stress, how you address you emotional, physical, social, and spiritual needs. Encourage others to share. Learn from each other. This organization is a family of sorts. Be a healthy functioning family that encourages and lifts each other.

This type of work requires healthy and strong support systems for which each individual is practicing healthy self-care, and the agency as a hole is practicing healthy support system dynamics. Always encourage each other with the importance of self-care and support. Help each other recognize when one of you is struggling, and encourage self-care and/or seeking help when the burdens get to heavy to bear on their own. Supervision, staffing, difficult cases, support, and counseling can only lead to a better, stronger agency because each individual is better and stronger. Support each other in the healthy evaluation of individual functioning.

Importance of Self-care when Working with Persons in Crisis

- Self-assessment – what needs are not being met
  - Know yourself
  - Evaluate yourself
- Seek supervision
- Seek support
- Seek Counseling

References

Amen, D. G. (2005). *Making a good brain great: The Amen clinic program for achieving and sustaining optimal mental performance.* New York, NY: Harmony Books.

American Psychiatric Association (2013). *Diagnostic and statistical manual of mental disorders* (5th ed.). Washington, DC: Author.

Aroche, J., Tukelija, S., & Askovic, M. (2009). Neurofeedback in work with refugee trauma: Rebuilding fragile foundations. *Biofeedback, 37*(2), 53-55. Retrieved from EbscoHost

Askovic, M., & Gould, D. (2009). Integration of neurofeedback in the therapeutic work with torture and trauma survivors: A case study. *Biofeedback, 37*(2). 56-62. Retrieved from EbscoHost

Bech, P., Olsen, L. R., Kjoller, M., & Rasmussen, N. K. (2003). Measuring well-being rather than the absence of distress symptoms: A comparison of the SF-36 Mental Health subscale and the WHO-five well-being scale. *International Journal of Methods in Psychiatric Research, 12*(2), 85-91. doi:10.1002/mpr.145

Braun, B. G. (1986). Issues in the psychotherapy of multiple personality disorder. In B. G. Braun (Ed.), *Treatment of multiple personality disorder* (pp. 3-28). Washington, DC: American Psychiatric Press.

Braun, B. G. (1988). The BASK Model of Dissociation. *Dissociation, 1*(1), 4-23.

Bremner, J. D. (2006). Traumatic stress: Effects on the brain. *Dialogues in Clinical Neuroscience, 8*(4), 445-461.

Bruhns, M. E. (2014). *From victim to survivor: A*

mixed methods investigation of the process of exiting and healing from commercial sexual exploitation in childhood. Retrieved from ProQuest Digital Dissertations. (UMI 3581158)

Burke, M. C. (2013). Complex trauma and severe forms of human trafficking: Implications for practice. In I. Koricanac (Ed.), *Human trafficking trauma and psychotherapy: Collection of paper.* Retrieved at http://europa.rs/images/publikacije/02-Human_Trafficking.pdf

Center on the Developing Child at Harvard University (2016). *From best practices to breakthrough impacts: A science-based approach to building a more promising future for young children and families.* Retrieved from www.developingchild.harvard.edu

Clawson, H. J., Dutch, N., Solomon, A., & Grace, L.
G. (2009). *Human trafficking into and within
the United States: A review of the literature.*
Retrieved from:
http://aspe.hhs.gov/hsp/07/HumanTrafficki
ng/

Clawson, H. J., Small, K. M., Go, E. S., & Myles, B.
W. (2003). *Needs assessment for service
providers and trafficking victims.* Fairfax, VA:
Caliber.

Cloitre, M. (1998). Sexual revictimization: Risk
factors and prevention. In V. M. Follette, J. I.
Ruzek, & F. R. Abueg (Eds.), Cognitive-
behavioral therapies for trauma (pp. 278–
304). New York, NY: Guilford Press.

Cloitre, M., Courtois, C. A., Charuvastra, A.,
Carapezza, R., Stolbach, B. C., & Green, B. L.
(2011). Treatment of complex PTSD: Results

of the ISTSS expert clinician survey on best practices. *Journal of Traumatic Stress, 24*(6), 615-627. doi:10.1002/jts.20697

Courtois, C. A., & Ford, J. D. (2012). *Treatment of complex trauma: A sequenced, relationship-based approach.* New York, NY: Guilford Press.

Cozolino, L. (2014). *The neuroscience of human relationships: Attachment and the developing social brain* (2nd ed.). New York, NY: W. W. Norton & Company.

DePrince, A.P. (2005). Social cognition and revictimization risk. *Journal of Trauma and Dissociation, 6,* 125-141.

De Wit, M., Pouwer, F., Gemke, R. J. B. J., Delemaare-van de Waal, H. A., & Snoek, F. J. (2007). Validation of the WHO-5 well-being index (WHO-5) in adolescents with type 1 diabetes. *Diabetes Care, 30*(8), 2003-2006.

English Oxford Living Dictionary (2017). *Emotional*

Intelligence

https://en.oxforddictionaries.com/definition

/emotional_intelligence

Edmond, T., Rubin, & A., Wambach, K. G. (1999).

The effectiveness of EMDR with adult

female survivors of childhood sexual abuse.

Social Work Research, 23(2), 103-127.

Retrieved from EbscoHost

Farley, M., Cotton, A., Lynne, J., Zumbeck, S.,

Spiwak, F., Reyes, M. E., & Sezgin, U. (2003).

Prostitution and trafficking in nine

countries: An update on violence and

posttraumatic stress disorder. *Journal of*

Trauma Practice, 2(3-4), 33-74.

Farley, M. (2009). Theory versus reality:

Commentary on four articles about

trafficking for prostitution. *Women's Studies*

International Forum, 32(4), 311-315.

Flowers, R. B. (2001). *Runaway kids and teenage prostitution: America's lost, abandoned, and sexually exploited children.* Westport, CT: Praeger Publishers.

Foa, E. & Rothbaum, B. O. (2001). *Treating the trauma of rape: Cognitive-behavioral therapy for PTSD.* New York, NY: Guilford Press.

Gajic-Veljanoski, O., & Stewart, D. E. (2007). Women trafficked into prostitution: Determinants, human rights and health needs. *Transcultural Psychiatry, 44,* 338-358. doi:10.1177/1363461507081635.

Goleman, D. (2011). *The brain and emotional intelligence: New insights.* Florence, MA: More Than Sound LLC.

Goodman, R. D., & Calderon, A. M. (2012). The use of mindfulness in trauma counseling.

Journal of Mental Health Counseling, 34(3), 254-268. Retrieved from EbscoHost

Granello, D. H., & Young, M. E. (2010). *Counseling today: Foundations of professional identity.* Upper Saddle River, NJ: Pearson Education.

Halvorsen, J. O. & Stenmark, H. (2010). Narrative exposure therapy for posttraumatic stress disorder in tortured refugees: A preliminary uncontrolled trial. *Scandinavian Journal of Psychology, 51*(1), 495-502. doi:10.1111/j.1467-9450.2010.00821.x

Haynes, N. E. (2015). Group art therapy using clay with victims of the sex trade. Retrieved from ProQuest Digital Dissertations. (1600052)

Herman, J. L. (1992). Complex PTSD: A syndrome in survivors of prolonged and repeated trauma. *Journal of Traumatic Stress, 5*(3), 377-391. doi:10.1002/jts.2490050305

Hickle, K. E., & Roe-Sepowitz, D. E. (2014). Putting the pieces back together: A group intervention for sexually exploited adolescent girls. *Social Work with Groups,* *37*(2), 99-113. doi:10.1080/01609513.2013.823838

Hien, D. A., Huiping, J., Campbell, A. N., Hu, M. C., Miele, G. M., Cohen, L. R., & . . . Nunes, E. V. (2010). Do treatment improvements in PTSD severity affect substance use outcomes? A secondary analysis from a randomized clinical trial in NIDA's clinical trials network. *The American Journal of Psychiatry, 167*(1), 95–101. doi:10.1176/appi.ajp.2009.09091261

Hodge, D. R. (2008). Sexual trafficking in the United States: A domestic problem with transnational dimensions. *Social Work, 53*(2),

143-152. doi:10.1093/sw/53.2.143

Hom, K., & Woods, S. (2013). Trauma and its aftermath for commercially sexually exploited women as told by front-line service providers. *Issues in Mental Health Nursing, 34*(1), 75-81.

Horsfall, J., Cleary, M., Hunt, G., & Walter, G. (2009). Psychosocial treatments for people with co-occurring severe mental illnesses and substance use disorders (dual diagnosis): A review of empirical evidence. *Harvard Review of Psychiatry, 17*(1), 24-34. doi:10.1080/10673220902724599

Jackson-Cherry, L. & Erford, B. T. (2014). *Crisis assessment, intervention and prevention,* (2nd ed.). Upper Saddle River, NJ: Pearson.

MacLean, P. D. (1952). Some psychiatric implications of physiological studies on frontotemporal portion of limbic system (visceral brain). *Electroencephalography and Clinical Neurophysiology, 4*(4), 407-418.

Macy, R. J., & Graham, L. M. (2012). Identifying domestic and international sex-trafficking victims during human service provision. *Trauma, Violence, and Abuse, 13*(2), 59-76. doi:10.1177/1524838012440340

Macy, R. J., & Johns, N. (2011). Aftercare services for international sex trafficking survivors: Informing U.S. service and program development in an emerging practice area. *Trauma, Violence, and Abuse, 12*(2), 87-98. doi:10.1177/1524838010390709

McFarlane, C. A., & Kaplan, A. (2012). Evidence-based psychological interventions for adult survivors of torture and trauma: A 30-year review. *Transcultural Psychiatry, 49*(3-4), 539-

657. doi:10.1177/1363461512447608

McHenry, B., Sikorski, A. M., & McHenry, J. (2014). *A counselor's introduction to neuroscience.* New York, NY: Routledge.

Mellin, E. A., Hunt, B., & Nichols, L. M. (2011). Counselor professional identity: Findings and implications for counseling and interprofessional collaboration. *Journal of Counseling and Development, 89*(2), 140-147.

Miller, E., Decker, M. R., Silverman, J. G., & Raj, A. (2007). Migration, sexual exploitation, and women's health: A case from a community health center. *Violence Against Women, 13,* 486-497. doi:10.1177/1077801207301614

Moroz, B. E. (2016, February). *Evaluating the efficacy of trauma-focused cognitive behavioral therapy and narrative exposure therapy with sex trafficking survivors.* Paper presented at the

Graduate Counseling Student Conference of
Virginia Association for Counselor
Education and Supervision (VACES),
Arlington, VA.

Muftic, L. R., & Finn, M. A. (2013). Health
outcomes among women trafficked for sex
in the United States: A closer look. *Journal of
Interpersonal Violence, 28*(9), 1859-1885.
doi:10.1177/0886260512469102

Ostrovschi, N. V., Prince, M. J., Zimmerman, C.,
Hotineanu, M. A., Gorceag, L. T., Gorceag, V.
I., . . . Abas, M. A. (2011). Women in posttrafficking services in Moldova: Diagnostic
interviews over two time periods to assess
returning women's mental health. *BMC
Public Health, 11*(232), 1-9. doi: 10.1186/1471-
2458-11-232

Rafferty, Y. (2008). The impact of trafficking on

children: Psychological and social policy

perspectives. *Child Development Perspectives*,

2(1), 13–18. doi:10.1111/j.1750-

8606.2008.00035.x

Rajmohan, V., & Mohandas, E. (2007). The limbic

system. *Indian Journal of Psychiatry, 49*(2),

132–139. doi:10.4103/0019-5545.33264

Raymond, J. G., & Hughes, D. M. (2001, April 17).

*Sex trafficking of women in the United States:

International and domestic trends*. Retrieved

from

https://www.ncjrs.gov/pdffiles1/nij/grants/18

7774.pdf

Reid, J. A. (2012). Exploratory review of route-

specific, gendered, and age-graded

dynamics of exploitation: Applying life

course theory to victimization in sex

trafficking in North America. *Aggression and*

Violent Behavior, 17, 257–271.

doi:10.1016/j.avb.2012.02.005

Roe-Sepowitz, D., Hickle, K., Cimno, A. (2012). The impact of abuse history and trauma symptoms on successful completion of a prostitution-exiting program. *Journal of Human Behavior on the Social Environment, 22,* 65-77.

Schauer, M., Neuner, F., & Elbert, T. (2005). *Narrative exposure therapy: A short term intervention for traumatic stress disorders after war, terror or torture.* Germany: Hogrefe & Huber.

Schrader, E. M., & Wendland, J. M. (2012). Music therapy programming at an aftercare center in Cambodia for survivors of child sexual exploitation and rape and their caregivers. *Social Work & Christianity, 39*(4), 390-406.

Retrieved from EbscoHost

Sherin, J. E., & Nemeroff, C. B. (2011). Post-traumatic stress disorder: The neurobiological impact of psychological trauma. *Dialogues in Clinical Neuroscience, 13*(3), 263-278.

Shonkoff, J. P., & Garner, A. S. (2011). The lifelong effects of early childhood adversity and toxic stress. *Pediatrics, (129)*1, 232-246. doi:10.1542/peds.2011-2663

Siskin, A., & Sun Wyler, L. (2013, February 19). *Trafficking in persons: U.S. policy and issues for congress.* Washington, DC: Congressional Research Service. Retrieved from https://www.fas.org/sgp/crs/row/RL34317.pdf

Slobodin, O., & de Jong, J. (2015). Mental health interventions for traumatized asylum seekers and refugees: What do we know

about their efficacy? *International Journal of

Social Psychiatry, 61*(1), 17-26.

doi:10.1177/0020764014535752

Spear, D. L. (2004). Human trafficking: A health

care perspective. *Association of Women's

Health Obstetric and Neonatal Nurses Lifelines,

8,* 314-321. doi:10.1177/1091592304269632

Tan, L. A. (2012). Art therapy with trafficked

women. *Therapy Today, 23*(5), 26-31.

Retrieved from EbscoHost

Tsutsumi, A., Izutsu, T., Poudyal, A. K., Kato, S., &

Marui, E. (2008). Mental health of female

survivors of human trafficking in Nepal.

Social Science & Medicine, 66(8), 1841-1847.

U.S. Department of State (2015, July). *Trafficking in

persons report.* Retrieved from

http://www.state.gov/documents/organizati

on/245365.pdf

Van Der Kol, B. (2014). *The Body Keeps the Score;*

brain, mind, and body in the healing of trauma.

NY. NY: Penguin Books ISBN 978-0-14-

312774-1

Williamson, E., Dutch, N. M., & Clawson, H. (2010).

Evidence-based mental health treatment for

victims of human trafficking. In *Study of*

HHS programs serving human trafficking

victims. Retrieved from

http://aspe.hhs.gov/basic-report/evidence-

based-mental-health-treatment-victims-

human-trafficking

Zimmerman, C., Hossain, M., Yun, K., Gajdadziev,

V., Guzun, N., Tchomarova, M., . . . Watts, C.

(2008). The health of trafficked women: A

survey of women entering posttrafficking

services in Europe. *American Journal of Public*

Health, 98(1), 55–59.

doi:10.2105/AJPH.2006.108357